EMMANUEL JOSEPH

The Green Imagination, How Art and Psychology Can Save the Planet

Contents

1 Chapter 1: The Call of the Green   1

2 Chapter 2: Art and the Ecological Mind   3

3 Chapter 3: The Healing Power of Nature-Inspired Art   5

4 Chapter 4: Eco-Art: A Movement for Change   7

5 Chapter 5: The Intersection of Psychology and Ecology   9

6 Chapter 6: The Power of Imagination   11

7 Chapter 7: Art and Environmental Education   12

8 Chapter 8: The Influence of Media and Pop Culture   14

9 Chapter 9: Art, Psychology, and Climate Change   16

10 Chapter 10: Sustainable Art Practices   18

11 Chapter 11: The Future of Green Creativity   19

12 Chapter 12: A Call to Action   20

13 Chapter 13: The Intersection of Science and Art   21

14 Chapter 14: Environmental Justice and Creative Expression   23

15 Chapter 15: The Global Art Movement for Sustainability   25

16 Chapter 16: The Healing Power of Community Art   27

17 Chapter 17: The Future of Environmental Art and Psychology   29

1

Chapter 1: The Call of the Green

An **Awakening** Picture a bustling cityscape where nature seems a distant memory. Amid the concrete jungle, an artist named Elisa finds herself disillusioned. The pollution and consumerism weigh heavily on her spirit. One morning, while painting in a local park, she experiences a profound connection with a tree. This moment of enlightenment sparks her journey towards using art to advocate for environmental conservation.

The Psychology of Connection The chapter dives into the psychological theories behind human connections with nature. From biophilia to eco-psychology, we explore how these concepts explain our innate affinity for the natural world. Elisa's story is interwoven with insights from psychologists who emphasize the importance of nurturing this bond for mental well-being.

Art as a Mirror to Nature Art has always reflected our relationship with nature. From ancient cave paintings to modern street art, creativity has been a medium for expressing environmental concerns. Through examples of iconic artworks, this section illustrates how art can inspire ecological consciousness and action.

Elisa's Green Movement Inspired by her awakening, Elisa starts a community project called "The Green Movement." She gathers like-minded artists, psychologists, and activists to create murals that depict the beauty and fragility of nature. These vibrant murals become a catalyst for change, drawing attention to environmental issues in the city.

Impact and Reflection As the murals gain popularity, the community begins to reflect on their own environmental impact. The chapter concludes with stories of individuals who were inspired by Elisa's project to adopt sustainable practices, highlighting the transformative power of art.

2

Chapter 2: Art and the Ecological Mind

The Role of Art in Shaping Beliefs Art has the power to shape societal beliefs and values. This chapter explores how art influences our perceptions of the environment. Through historical and contemporary examples, we see how artists have used their work to challenge ecological ignorance and promote sustainable living.

Case Study: The Forest Guardians In a remote village, a group of artists known as the Forest Guardians create sculptures from recycled materials. Their art not only beautifies the landscape but also educates the community about the importance of conservation. The chapter delves into their journey and the impact of their work.

The Psychology of Persuasion Understanding the psychological principles of persuasion, such as cognitive dissonance and social proof, is crucial for effective environmental advocacy. This section discusses how these principles can be harnessed through art to encourage sustainable behavior.

Interactive Art and Community Engagement Interactive art installations, like eco-friendly sculptures and community gardens, engage people on a deeper level. Elisa collaborates with the Forest Guardians to create an interactive art trail that educates visitors about local flora and fauna. The success of this project underscores the power of collective creativity.

A New Perspective The chapter wraps up with personal stories from visitors of the art trail, who share how the experience changed their

3

perspectives on nature and inspired them to make eco-friendly choices. These anecdotes highlight the ripple effect of art-driven ecological awareness.

3

Chapter 3: The Healing Power of Nature-Inspired Art

Art Therapy and Environmental Stress Nature-inspired art can be a therapeutic tool for alleviating environmental stress. This chapter introduces us to Sarah, a therapist who uses nature-themed art sessions to help her clients cope with eco-anxiety. Sarah's innovative approach provides a new avenue for mental health support.

Eco-Anxiety: A Growing Concern Eco-anxiety is a real and growing concern, especially among young people. The chapter examines the psychological impact of environmental degradation and how nature-inspired art can serve as a coping mechanism.

Art Workshops in Nature Sarah organizes art workshops in natural settings, allowing participants to draw inspiration directly from their surroundings. These workshops become a sanctuary for individuals seeking solace from the pressures of modern life. The chapter details the transformative experiences of participants.

Case Study: Healing through Creativity We follow the story of John, a teenager grappling with eco-anxiety. Through Sarah's art workshops, John finds a way to channel his fears into creative expression. His journey illustrates the profound healing power of nature-inspired art.

A Path to Recovery The chapter concludes with the broader implications of art therapy for environmental stress. Through stories of transformation, we see how art can be a powerful tool for fostering emotional resilience and a deeper connection to nature.

4

Chapter 4: Eco-Art: A Movement for Change

The Rise of Eco-Art Eco-art is an emerging movement that combines artistic expression with environmental activism. This chapter explores the origins of eco-art and its growing influence on global environmental discourse.

Case Study: The Plastic Ocean An eco-artist named Maya creates installations using plastic waste collected from the ocean. Her work highlights the devastating impact of plastic pollution on marine life. Through Maya's story, we learn about the challenges and triumphs of eco-artists.

The Art of Advocacy Eco-art goes beyond aesthetics; it's a powerful tool for advocacy. The chapter discusses how artists like Maya use their work to raise awareness, inspire action, and influence policy changes. We explore the strategies that make eco-art an effective medium for environmental advocacy.

Community Engagement through Art Maya's installations spark community-wide clean-up efforts and educational programs. The chapter highlights the importance of community engagement in the success of eco-art initiatives. Stories of collective action demonstrate the potential for art to drive social change.

A Vision for the Future The chapter ends with a vision for the future of eco-art. Through interviews with emerging eco-artists, we glimpse the innovative ideas and projects that are shaping the movement. The chapter leaves readers inspired to support and participate in eco-art initiatives.

5

Chapter 5: The Intersection of Psychology and Ecology

Understanding Ecological Psychology Ecological psychology examines the relationship between humans and their environments. This chapter introduces key concepts and theories that shed light on how our surroundings influence our behavior and well-being.

The Role of Art in Ecological Psychology Art plays a crucial role in ecological psychology by shaping our perceptions and interactions with the environment. The chapter explores how art can be used to promote ecological awareness and foster sustainable behavior.

Case Study: The Urban Green Project In a densely populated city, a group of psychologists and artists collaborate on the Urban Green Project. Their goal is to create green spaces and public art installations that encourage residents to connect with nature. The chapter follows their journey and the impact of their work.

Behavioral Insights for Environmental Action Understanding human behavior is key to promoting environmental action. The chapter discusses how insights from behavioral psychology can inform the design of art and interventions that encourage sustainable practices.

A Call to Action The chapter concludes with a call to action for readers to integrate the principles of ecological psychology into their own lives.

Through stories of individuals who have made meaningful changes, we see the potential for collective impact.

6

Chapter 6: The Power of Imagination

Imagination as a Catalyst for Change Imagination is a powerful tool for envisioning a sustainable future. This chapter explores how imaginative thinking can inspire innovative solutions to environmental challenges.

The Role of Artists and Creatives Artists and creatives play a crucial role in shaping our visions of the future. The chapter highlights the contributions of visionary artists who use their creativity to advocate for environmental sustainability.

Case Study: The Green City Initiative A collective of artists, architects, and urban planners come together to reimagine a city as a green utopia. Their innovative designs and concepts demonstrate the potential for art and imagination to drive urban sustainability.

The Psychology of Visionary Thinking Understanding the psychology behind visionary thinking can help us harness our own creative potential. The chapter discusses strategies for cultivating imaginative thinking and applying it to environmental problems.

Building a Sustainable Future The chapter concludes with a vision for a sustainable future, inspired by the imaginative work of artists and creatives. Through stories of hope and innovation, readers are encouraged to dream big and take action towards a greener world.

7

Chapter 7: Art and Environmental Education

The Role of Art in Education Art can be a powerful tool for environmental education. This chapter explores how art-based approaches can enhance our understanding of ecological issues and inspire action.

Case Study: The Eco-Art School A progressive school integrates eco-art into its curriculum, teaching students about environmental sustainability through creative projects. The chapter follows the experiences of students and teachers who embrace this innovative approach.

Engaging the Next Generation Engaging young people in environmental education is crucial for building a sustainable future. The chapter discusses strategies for using art to capture the interest and imagination of the next generation.

The Impact of Creative Learning Creative learning experiences can have a lasting impact on students. The chapter shares stories of students who have been inspired by eco-art projects to pursue careers in environmental advocacy.

A Blueprint for Education The chapter concludes with a blueprint for integrating art and environmental education. Through practical advice and success stories, readers are encouraged to adopt creative approaches in their own educational contexts.

8

Chapter 8: The Influence of Media and Pop Culture

Media as a Catalyst for Change Media and pop culture have a significant influence on public perception and behavior. This chapter explores how environmental themes in movies, TV shows, music, and social media can inspire a global audience to take action for the planet.

Case Study: The Eco-Superhero Phenomenon A popular superhero franchise introduces an eco-conscious character who fights to protect the environment. The chapter delves into the impact of this character on fans, especially younger viewers, and how it sparks interest in environmental issues.

Music with a Message Musicians have long used their platform to address social and environmental issues. Through the stories of artists who incorporate environmental themes into their music, we see how melodies and lyrics can resonate with audiences and drive change.

Social Media and Environmental Advocacy Social media platforms offer a powerful tool for spreading environmental messages. The chapter examines successful campaigns and viral content that have mobilized communities around the world to participate in environmental activism.

The Cultural Shift As more media and pop culture icons embrace environmental advocacy, a cultural shift occurs. The chapter concludes with stories of individuals who were inspired by media to make sustainable choices, highlighting the transformative power of pop culture.

9

Chapter 9: Art, Psychology, and Climate Change

The **Psychological Impact of Climate Change** Climate change has profound psychological effects, including feelings of helplessness and anxiety. This chapter explores these impacts and how art can be a therapeutic outlet for processing climate-related emotions.

Art as a Tool for Climate Communication Communicating the complexities of climate change can be challenging. The chapter discusses how art can simplify and humanize these issues, making them more relatable and compelling to a wider audience.

Case Study: The Climate Canvas Project A collaborative project called the Climate Canvas brings together artists and scientists to create murals depicting the effects of climate change. The chapter follows the journey of the project and the powerful messages conveyed through the art.

Building Resilience through Creativity Art can help build emotional and psychological resilience in the face of climate change. The chapter shares stories of individuals who have found strength and inspiration through creative expression, demonstrating the importance of resilience in environmental activism.

A Global Perspective Climate change is a global issue that requires collective action. The chapter concludes with stories of international art collaborations that address climate change, highlighting the power of art to unite people across borders.

10

Chapter 10: Sustainable Art Practices

The Art of Sustainability Sustainable art practices focus on minimizing the environmental impact of creative processes. This chapter explores the principles and techniques of sustainable art, from using eco-friendly materials to reducing waste.

Case Study: The Zero-Waste Studio An artist named Leo transforms his studio into a zero-waste space, using recycled materials and sustainable techniques. The chapter follows Leo's journey and the innovative methods he adopts to create environmentally friendly art.

Eco-Friendly Materials and Techniques The chapter delves into the use of sustainable materials and techniques in art. Through examples of artists who prioritize eco-friendly practices, we learn about the benefits and challenges of sustainable creativity.

The Role of Technology Technology can play a crucial role in promoting sustainable art practices. The chapter discusses how digital tools and innovations are helping artists reduce their environmental footprint and create impactful work.

A Movement for Change The chapter concludes with stories of artists who are leading the sustainable art movement. Their commitment to eco-friendly practices inspires readers to consider the environmental impact of their own creative endeavors.

11

Chapter 11: The Future of Green Creativity

Innovations in Green Art The future of green creativity is filled with exciting innovations. This chapter explores cutting-edge ideas and projects that are pushing the boundaries of sustainable art and design. **Case Study: The Solar-Powered Art Installation** A groundbreaking art installation powered entirely by solar energy captivates audiences and demonstrates the potential of renewable energy in art. The chapter delves into the creation and impact of this innovative project.

The Intersection of Art and Technology As technology continues to evolve, new possibilities emerge for green creativity. The chapter discusses how advancements in technology are enabling artists to create more sustainable and impactful work.

Collaborative Creativity Collaboration is key to the future of green creativity. The chapter highlights projects that bring together artists, scientists, and communities to address environmental challenges through creative solutions.

A Vision for Tomorrow The chapter concludes with a vision for the future of green creativity. Through stories of visionary artists and innovators, readers are inspired to imagine and create a more sustainable world.

12

Chapter 12: A Call to Action

The Power of Individual Action Every individual has the power to make a difference. This chapter emphasizes the importance of personal responsibility and the impact of small, everyday actions on the environment.

Case Study: The Eco-Art Activists A group of passionate individuals known as the Eco-Art Activists use their creative talents to advocate for environmental sustainability. The chapter follows their journey and the ways in which their art inspires change.

Building Sustainable Communities Communities play a crucial role in fostering environmental sustainability. The chapter discusses how art can bring people together and create a sense of shared purpose in addressing ecological challenges.

Inspiring Future Generations The chapter explores the importance of inspiring future generations to care for the planet. Through stories of young eco-artists and activists, readers are encouraged to support and nurture the next generation of environmental stewards.

A Green Imagination The book concludes with a reflection on the power of imagination to create a sustainable future. Through the stories and insights shared throughout the book, readers are inspired to embrace their creativity and take action for the planet.

13

Chapter 13: The Intersection of Science and Art

Bridging the Gap The intersection of science and art offers a unique perspective on environmental issues. This chapter explores how these two fields can collaborate to promote ecological awareness and innovation.

Case Study: The Bio-Art Lab In a cutting-edge laboratory, scientists and artists work together on bio-art projects that highlight the beauty and complexity of nature. The chapter delves into the fascinating world of bio-art and its potential to inspire environmental stewardship.

Artistic Representation of Scientific Data Art can make scientific data more accessible and engaging. The chapter discusses how artists use creative visualization techniques to communicate complex environmental data, making it more relatable to the public.

The Power of Collaboration Collaboration between scientists and artists can lead to groundbreaking innovations. The chapter shares stories of successful collaborations that have resulted in impactful environmental projects.

A New Paradigm The chapter concludes with a vision for a future where science and art work hand in hand to address ecological challenges. Through stories of pioneering projects, readers are inspired to embrace interdisciplinary collaboration.

14

Chapter 14: Environmental Justice and Creative Expression

The Intersection of Art and Activism Art has a long history of being a powerful tool for activism. This chapter explores the role of art in promoting environmental justice and advocating for marginalized communities.

Case Study: The Environmental Justice Mural Project In a diverse urban neighborhood, artists create murals that highlight the environmental injustices faced by their community. The chapter follows the journey of the project and its impact on raising awareness and driving change.

Amplifying Voices through Art Art can amplify the voices of marginalized communities and bring attention to their struggles. The chapter shares stories of artists who use their work to advocate for environmental justice and social equity.

The Role of Psychology in Environmental Justice Understanding the psychological impacts of environmental injustices is crucial for effective advocacy. The chapter discusses how insights from psychology can inform art-based approaches to promoting environmental justice.

A Call to Action The chapter concludes with a call to action for readers to support environmental justice initiatives. Through stories of successful advocacy, readers are encouraged to use their creativity to drive positive change.

Chapter 15: The Global Art Movement for Sustainability

Art for a Global Audience The global art movement for sustainability connects artists from around the world in a shared mission to protect the planet. This chapter explores the power of art to transcend cultural boundaries and unite people in the fight for environmental sustainability.

Case Study: The Global Eco-Art Exhibition An international eco-art exhibition showcases the work of artists from diverse backgrounds, each addressing unique environmental issues. The chapter delves into the stories behind the artworks and the impact of the exhibition on global audiences.

Cultural Perspectives on Environmentalism Different cultures have unique perspectives on environmentalism. The chapter discusses how artists incorporate their cultural heritage into their work, creating a rich tapestry of global environmental art.

The Role of Technology in Global Collaboration Technology plays a crucial role in facilitating global collaboration among artists. The chapter explores how digital platforms and tools enable artists to connect, share ideas, and collaborate on environmental projects.

A Vision for a Sustainable World The chapter concludes with a vision for a sustainable world, inspired by the global art movement. Through stories of international collaboration and innovation, readers are encouraged to join the global effort to protect the planet.

26

16

Chapter 16: The Healing Power of Community Art

The **Role of Art in Community Building** Art can bring communities together and foster a sense of shared purpose. This chapter explores how community art projects promote environmental sustainability and strengthen social bonds.

Case Study: The Community Garden Mural In a small town, residents come together to create a mural in their community garden. The chapter follows the journey of the project and its impact on fostering community spirit and promoting sustainable practices.

Art as a Tool for Social Healing Art can help heal social divisions and build bridges between diverse groups. The chapter shares stories of community art projects that have brought people together to address environmental challenges.

The Psychology of Community Engagement Understanding the psychology of community engagement is crucial for the success of art-based initiatives. The chapter discusses how insights from psychology can inform the design and implementation of community art projects.

A Blueprint for Community Action The chapter concludes with practical advice for readers interested in starting their own community art projects. Through stories of successful initiatives, readers are inspired to use art as a tool for building sustainable and resilient communities.

28

17

Chapter 17: The Future of Environmental Art and Psychology

Emerging Trends in Environmental Art The field of environmental art is constantly evolving. This chapter explores emerging trends and innovative practices that are shaping the future of environmental art.

The Role of Psychology in Shaping the Future Psychology plays a crucial role in understanding and addressing environmental challenges. The chapter discusses how insights from psychology can inform the future of environmental art and advocacy.

Innovations in Eco-Friendly Art Practices Artists are constantly finding new ways to create eco-friendly art. The chapter shares stories of innovative practices and techniques that are pushing the boundaries of sustainable creativity.

A Vision for the Future The book concludes with a vision for the future of environmental art and psychology. Through stories of pioneering artists and psychologists, readers are inspired to imagine and create a more sustainable and harmonious world.

In **"The Green Imagination: How Art and Psychology Can Save the Planet,"** journey into a world where creativity meets environmental consciousness. This inspiring book reveals how art and psychology can unite to foster a more sustainable and harmonious planet.

Through 17 engaging chapters, readers are introduced to visionary artists, psychologists, and activists who use their talents to advocate for ecological well-being. From interactive murals and eco-art installations to nature-inspired therapy sessions and global art movements, each chapter is filled with fascinating stories and practical insights.

Discover how art can reflect our connection with nature, influence societal beliefs, and promote sustainable practices. Explore the psychological theories that explain our bond with the environment and learn how imaginative thinking can inspire innovative solutions to ecological challenges.

"The Green Imagination" delves into the transformative power of community art projects, the role of media and pop culture in environmental advocacy, and the healing effects of nature-themed art. It also highlights emerging trends in sustainable art practices and the importance of interdisciplinary collaboration between artists and scientists.

Packed with real-life case studies and visionary perspectives, this book is a call to action for individuals and communities to harness their creativity and take meaningful steps towards a greener world. Whether you're an artist, psychologist, educator, or environmental enthusiast, "The Green Imagination" will leave you inspired to make a difference.